C000262439

I KICK
THEREFORE
I AM

RONNIE MATTHEWS

I KICK THEREFORE I AM

THE LITTLE BOOK OF PREMIER LEAGUE WISDOM

BLOOMSBURY

LONDON · NEW DELHI · NEW YORK · SYDNEY

First published in 2012
Bloomsbury Publishing Plc
50 Bedford Square
London WC1B 3DP
www.bloomsbury.com

ISBN 978 1 4088 3276 9

A CIP catalogue record for this book is available from the British Library.

10 9 8 7 6 5 4 3 2 1

Typeset in Ronnie Electric and Ronnie Showboat.
Printed and bound in Great Britain by the MPG Books Group.

WE ARE ALL IN
THE GUTTER, BUT
SOME OF US ARE
SHOOTING FOR
THE STARS

RON'S A WRONG-UN
DO-RON SHOE BONG
RON GONE!
MORE RON MORON
YA-DO-WRONG-RON
GOING... GOING... RON...
ONE TON RON
SING-A-LONG-A WRONG-RON
RONNIE CROCKS FOX IN BOX SHOCK
DA WHO RON-RON?

WHO is Ronnie Matthews? A footballer, a fighter, a lover of life, a man who has been to the brink and back. A hero? To some, yes. The face that shamed football? To the newspapers, maybe. The truth is probably somewhere in between.

Football has been good to me but, as I come to the end of my playing days, I realise a man is more than the games he has played, the goals he has scored, the cars he has crashed, the phone numbers of Nuts cover girls he has had in his phone (six – seven if you count Jordan and Katie Price as two people which to be fair she has earned the right to do).

This book is about football, but it's also about my other passions: fashion, philosophy, art, dogs, my kids, my missus Tonette. It's been an incredible journey for a lad who was nearly thrown out of Watford Schoolboys for having bilaterally degraded feet, and I want to share it with you.

Welcome to the world of Ronnie Matthews. Enjoy.

RONNIE ON...

FOOTBALL

IN 16 years of football, I've known incredible highs on the field. And incredible highs off it, too, before I got myself straightened out. Top moment? When I walked out at Wembley. My heart swelled just to be on the same pitch as those legends. Theakston. Ramsay. That guy who's mates with Robbie Williams. Cheryl Baker in the Makelele role. I'd arrived. Sure, the call-up to Soccer Aid came at the 11th hour, but when Ronnie Matthews has a chance to do his bit for African kiddies AND hang with some of the biggest celebrities working in Britain today, it's very much a case of: have boots, will travel.

Of course, there have been lows as well: injury, arrests, being told I was too fat to play for the Crawley Old Red Lion just 18 months after being capped for England. Rock bottom was my last game here before I moved to Turkey. Playing for Peterborough v Watford, a fox got on the pitch and was charging around all over the shop. It nicked the ball away from me just as I was going in for a 50-50 with Big Martin Taylor and I've ended up catching the fox two-footed. The ref had the red card out right away and I became the first British player to be sent off for a professional foul on an animal. Looking at the replays I still say the fox made a meal of the challenge.

The physio came on to have a look at the fox and I said maybe they should put a green tent around it like at the Grand National, only they didn't have a green tent, so Barry Fry had to hold a copy of the Daily Star over the animal to like shield it from the crowd's eyes, and eventually they took it off on the stretcher.

I'd be lying if I said I enjoyed seeing the front pages the next day – a new low for football blah blah blah – never mind explaining to my little princess Ginseng and Ronnie Junior that Daddy had put a fox out the game for six weeks with a two-footed challenge.

But that's football for you. One minute you're exchanging one-twos and bedroom war stories about Amanda Holden with Neil Morrissey, next minute you're public enemy number one for the nation's animal rights nutters.

WRITING

OBVIOUSLY there's been loads of books about philosophy and religion and the big questions of life. And millions that are about a person's life story. But I don't think there's ever been a book before that does both at the same time… until now! If this book was a footballer, it would be in the Teddy Sheringham role: creative vision but also an eye for goal and great in the air, as well as probably shagging a Big Brother contestant or two in its younger days, although obviously that's behind this book now that it's happily married.

When I told people that I wanted to write a book a lot of them said it couldn't be done. Well, if there's one thing you don't want to say to Ronnie Matthews if you don't want him to do something it's to say it can't be done. Don't do that, because he'll do it.

So how do you write a book? Three words: iPad. Ideas. Ikea. I got my agent to put me in the shop window with a few publishers, I signed a book deal, and then I got myself on the North Circular and I went to Ikea and I bought myself a desk. I already had a file saved in my iPad, and loads of ideas, so once Tonette had assembled the desk and we'd moved Ronnie Junior out of his bedroom, I had a place to work, something to write on and there was no stopping me.

A lot of footballers use books to settle scores. Not me. I think the world knows quite enough about how badly I was treated by David O'Leary, and I'm just not the sort of snide bloke that's going to bear a grudge. I'm sure one day that somebody might give David another chance to manage a football club and he'll have nothing but support from me if and when he does. And this is not the sort of book where I'll be betraying confidences and spreading gossip so, Kammy: relax mate, there was no way you could have known the maid was going to walk in and, let's face it, at a Premier Inn in Northallerton they probably see stuff like that all the time.

No gossip. No grudges. Just my thoughts, my beliefs, my stories, my life, my hopes, my dreams and my top ten best-ever meals I've had in a Harvester.

FAME

MIND THE PAPS

DEFINITELY one of the best things about being a footballer is that it opens up doors and you get to meet top people from all other walks of life. I've been lucky enough to become close personal friends with some brilliant celebrities, including:

Neil and Christine Hamilton – the cleverest couple I have ever met

Jodie Marsh – still well fit even though she's got thighs like Roberto Carlos these days

Stuart Pearce's brother Dennis – although don't get him started on politics

Phil and Grant Mitchell – both a hell of a lot nicer in real life

British women's tennis legend Elena Baltacha – brilliant value on the golf course

Tim Lovejoy – obviously

All five of Steps – although to be fair H and I have since fallen out

Diana Ross – legend. We're working on her penalty tekkers!

That guy from Big Brother series six – the one who got off with that bird in the Jacuzzi

Norman St John-Stevas – he was like a second grandfather to me, I was gutted when he died

DOGS

ON the face of it, Roy Keane and I haven't got a lot in common. Keano was very much a 110% man, even more than that on the big European nights, and I was what you might call more of an artist. A creator, not a destroyer. Brahma to Roy's Shiva, if you like. And where Roy was very much in your face 24-7 for the whole 90 minutes, I admit I did tend to drift in and out of games. And in and out of clubs as well, come to think of it. But Roy and me do share two things: neither of us can stick Mick McCarthy, and we're both famous for our love of dogs.

Come rain or shine, you'll find Ronnie Matthews up bright and early (unless I've had a late one, in which case Tonette steps in) to walk his two best friends. I've got a Doberman, Baresi, and a Staffordshire Bull Terrier-Chihuahua cross called Nintendo. The kids named him. There wasn't a lot I could do about it. The Stafforhuahua is a big personality in a small, very aggressive dog. Pound-for-pound, relative to their size, they have the biggest willies of any breed. Not a lot of people know that until I tell them.

When I'm walking the dogs out in the woods behind our house, I feel free and at one with nature. Just man and beast, prowling, running, hunting. It does wonders for clearing your mind and grounding you. On the way back, we'll hop over the dual carriageway and have a cheeky fry-up in the Little Chef. At first I had to pretend to be blind so as I could take the dogs into the restaurant area, but after a few weeks the duty manager admitted that he'd recognised me and they were turning a blind eye, if you'll pardon the pun, on account of my celebrity status. Also, the early shift waitress Sunita was worried that Nintendo might turn nasty if she got too close. Fair enough. Upshot was, I can sit in peace and quiet in the corner of the Little Chef, enjoying an Early Starter breakfast with extra hash brown, my two dogs by my side under the table, and I start each day feeling like the king of the world.

GOD

THE Big Man.

The Chief.

The Gaffer in The Sky.

Does Ronnie Matthews believe in God?

Does God believe in Ronnie Matthews?

Is there an all-knowing deity-type figure governing all that we do, like Ferguson at United?

Or is he more of a live-and-let-live sort of God who trusts us to have free will and take responsibility for our own decisions, like Gordon Strachan when he let us go golfing the day before that Cup quarter-final?

← GO

Nietzsche said that God is dead.

But what if he's only sleeping, like one of the Sheffield teams or a Nottingham Forest?

The way I see it on God: the jury's out, so why dive in and commit yourself? Because it's like Merse used to say: 'it's better to have an each way bet than do all your dough because your odds-on cert got brought down by a loose horse in the 3.20 at Wincanton.' To be fair to Merse, he wasn't very good at gambling, but the theological point stands irregardless.

HAND
OF →
GOD

LOVE

RONNIE Matthews is full of love. Here are the types of love that you can be filled up of.

Love for football

Love for your nan

Love for the badge (can change but probably worth kissing first and asking questions later)

Love for a racehorse

Peter Ndlovu (top man)

Love you feel for the lads after a big win and you're all in the bath

Love for Ronnie Junior and my little princess Ginseng

Groovy kind of love (massive respect to Phil Collins)

Love for your wife

Love for your girlfriend

Ladies Love Ladies IX (definitely in my top five films ever seen)

IN my time, I've been guilty of all seven deadly sins: lust, greed, pride, and the rest – often all in one night out with the lads at Faces! But to be serious: one vice has cost me badly throughout my life.

ANGER

Whether it's been handbags at ten paces in a kebab shop or that aggravated assault charge at Carrow Road – which I still say would of gone away quietly if Delia could have kept her mouth shut – the red mist has been a constant monkey on my back. But if I learned one thing in prison in Turkey, other than how to make alcoholic hummus in a radiator, it was that anger is a negative emotion that only harms the person who expresses it. Big Ergun taught me that as soon as I got there, and I definitely never expressed anger to Ergun a second time. I owe that bloke a lot.

Nowadays if I feel anger coming over me on the pitch or off it, I just count up to 24. Why 24, not ten, you ask? That's the number of red cards I've had in my career, and also the number of months the judge promised me if I 'appear before him again', as he called it, at Watford Magistrates Court. The thought of being inside again with Big Ergun or the English equivalent is enough to make the anger float away like a balloon. I've been very blessed.

THE PRESS—THE PRESS

IF you ask any player, they'll tell you that the biggest cancer facing the game today is the press. I've lost count of the number of stories they've made up about me.

'Ronnie Matthews stumbles out of club drunk at 3am'. It was 2.30, actually, and how was I supposed to know that Ledley King would be lying on the pavement? I tripped over the big man: it could have happened to anyone, sober or drunk.

They should think about people's families: it's not right my kids read that paper and see me sprawled all over the pavement, while Ledley comes out smelling of roses, and Tennessee Fried Chicken, kipping safe and sound in the gutter out of shot.

Or how about 'Barry Fry sells Ronnie Matthews to Turkish strugglers for bag of tracksuits and a rug?' Insulting. That carpet was beautiful. Priceless, Barry told me. He washes his dogs on it to this day and, believe me, if you know Barry, there's no higher praise than that.

And of course, in these days of camera phones, everyone's a photo-journalist now. You can't even have a blazing row with the wife in Nandos without some little smartarse uploading a clip to Youface or whatever it is they do.

THE PRESS—THE PRESS

Lazy journalists will just make up any old rubbish for money. It sickens me. When I first got my column on 'The News Of The World' I wanted to address that very issue, but they didn't want to know. I saw the writing was on the wall for the so-called newspaper industry a while ago, when they told me cutbacks were getting so tight on the paper me and Neil Ruddock would have to ghost-write each other's columns to save on costs.

You wouldn't know it to look at him, but Razor's a real stickler for spelling – after Lynne Truss made a right mug of him on pro-celebrity Countdown for Great Ormond Street – and we fell out on more than one occasion.

To help them out on the paper, I said they could hack my phone if they wanted, throw them a juicy gossip bone or two so to speak. But once again they thought they knew better and told me thanks but no thanks. I can't say as I was surprised when it all got shut down.

SAM, 23 (36-23-34)

TRANSFERS

I'VE had more than my fair share of transfers, but I'm proud to say I never moved away from a club for money, apart from at Crewe when the chairman wrote me a personal cheque if I agreed to leave during pre-season, no questions asked. Here's my career moves so far:

YTS forms at Watford. Make my debut on Valentine's Day 1996 under Glenn Roeder. He is sacked immediately after the game, coincidentally. Play a few games that season. Watford relegated.

In 1999, the big one: I am sold to Leeds United, becoming Britain's first million-pound-utility player. Sadly it never really works out for me at it is a tough time for me, going on loan, anywhere I can get a game to be fair. At one stage, I am on loan at three different clubs at once; and during a Johnstone's Paint game I actually play the first 45 minutes for one team, change shirts at halftime and come out in a false beard to play for the opposition in the second half.

2010 A new hope: Barry Fry buys me for Peterborough.

2011 Barry offloads me to Trabzonspor. Turkey is a nightmare from start to finish.

2012 Released from prison in Turkey, and back in the UK ready to get my career kick-started.

...cases, what with the various court cases and the fact that Lee Bowyer is blocking my way into the first team and often into the carpark as well. Wind-up merchant. The final straw is when I'm caught setting Bowyer's car on fire after training.

2002 Sold to Southampton. Probably the happiest times of my career: regular first-team football, and I open up a chip shop.

2004 Harry Redknapp arrives at Southampton, sells me to Portsmouth. The fans aren't happy. Nor am I.

2005 Effing Redknapp arrives at Portsmouth; sells me back to Southampton. But the magic has gone, and I'm soon on my way out of St Mary's.

2006 At Middlesbrough under Steve McClaren. I catch his eye, he is brilliant for me. Sadly miss the second half of the season after I catch miner's lung. My Southern constitution can't handle the smog.

2007 Steve leaves to manage England and gives me my cap against the Faroe Islands. Sold by Boro to Hartlepool soon after.

2008 Doesn't really click for me at Hartlepool. The next two years a bit of a mess: Gillingham, Crewe, Crawley Town, Crawley City, Old Red Lion (Crawley), Celtic, Hartlepool, St Albans, Fradley, and Allihfe1, Lee

FAMILY

PETERBOROUGH v Plymouth. August 2010.
I was stood on the touchline, hoping Barry Fry
would bring me on, but me and Barry were in
one of our periods of not talking to each other.
(I'd covered his XJS in shaving foam; he's locked
me in the London Road caretaker's cupboard
over the Bank Holiday weekend.) He told me to
bugger off and warm up in front of the away fans.
The Plymouth fans chanted 'Who are ya? Who
are ya?' at me. When our own fans joined in,
that was hurtful. But it got me thinking: who is
Ronnie Matthews?

Who is Ronnie Matthews? Where did he come
from? Where did he go? I knew I had to learn
more about my family past to be part of my own
present in future. When the call came from ITV
Central to appear on 'What Does He Think He
Is?' I jumped at the chance. With the help of the
programme, I traced my family all the way back
to 1935. They never ended up using my story in
the end because some of the stuff Nan had done
could still have gone to court. But it opened my
eyes, and I don't plan on closing them any time
soon.

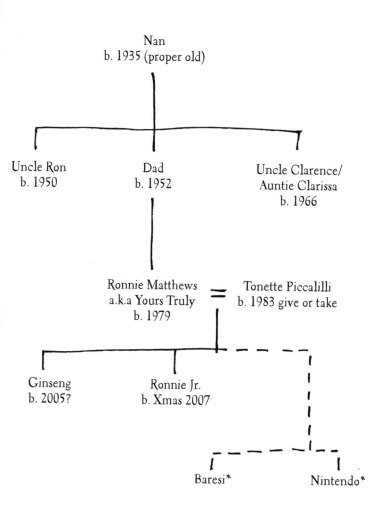

THE GEAR

GOLDEN BOOTS

WHEN I was at Leeds I got them to make these with actual gold leaf on the inners but the lads kept melting them down.

JOCKSTRAP

XXXL – 'nuff said!

They retired this for me when I left Crawley.
'No one at the club wants to see that number on
the pitch ever again,' the gaffer said.

PREPARATION

ROUTINE is vital for a professional athlete. You have to run through your drills, get yourself ready, give yourself the best possible chance to succeed. Before every game, I always do exactly the same preparation:

- ✓ Wake up – nice and early

- ✓ Have sex – focuses the mind, relaxes you, ensures no embarrassing boner in the showers

- ✓ If sex not a option (away game or Tonette headache) – get on the internet

- ✓ Pasta – something low-fat, with chicken. If weather cold: lasagne and chips

- ✓ Get to ground – listen to 'Now That's What I Call Buddhist Chanting' in the car

- ✓ Get corner of changing room – vital to minimise pranks

- ✓ Bants – piss in goalkeeper's shoe. Bit of a superstition for me, this

- ✓ Change into kit – left sock on first, then right shoe. Right shoe off, right sock on. Then left shoe. Finally right shoe

- ✔ Turn lights on and off – 144 times exactly (check no teammates have epilepsy; had a nasty incident with this at Colchester once)
- ✔ Bowel movement – self-explanatory really
- ✔ Pre-match doughnut – jam if possible, Krispy Kreme ideal
- ✔ Have a bet – telephone bookies usually
- ✔ Get psyched up – pick a fight with a teammate, manager, tea lady etc
- ✔ Bowel movement
- ✔ Doughnut
- ✔ READY TO ROCK AND ROLL!!!

WEE

SHOE

MARRIAGE

LIKE a great forward pair, a marriage is a partnership. You've got your big man who puts himself about a bit, makes a nuisance of himself and knocks it down to a nippy little feller who pops up and says 'thanks very much' – bang! 1-0!

Obviously in most marriages you have a bloke and a woman, and not a big bloke and a little bloke – although obviously in this day and age that's getting more and more common. Not that I've got anything against it myself as long as it doesn't cause bad feeling in the dressing room. The point is: marriage is a partnership.

My own marriage to the lovely Tonette has endured its ups and downs, but I am very lucky in that she has been a model wife. I mean that literally: she did a lot of modelling (catalogue, tasteful swimwear, no open-leg) before she decided to hang up her boots at the grand old age of 21 and concentrate 110% on raising Ginseng and Ronnie Junior.

Have we had our points of disagreement? Sure. But once she had her lawyer go through the pre-nup properly, she realised that things were crystal clear as a bell, and it's been an open road ever since.

So that's my advice on marriage: be respectful of each other, read the small print, and never go to bed angry – especially not with someone other than the wife.

BUSINESS

ONE of my biggest mates in football has always been Rio Ferdinand. Like me, Rio is a guy who loves his football but realises that there is more to life than just being a top player. Last summer, I had an incredible idea for a chain of restaurants and I asked Rio if he wanted to come in with me. The concept was to take the best of British grub but put it together with sexy, modern food. Rio got it right away, and told me that he knew a couple of guys who would also be up for having an investment dibble.

So Rio, Ashley Cole, Jay-Z and me are ready to launch UK Sushi. Ashley's suggestion was, you know like in Yo Sushi, where the food comes round on those little plates, but we'd take it to another level: the chefs would sit on a conveyor belt and come round and cook your food at the table.

I loved it; especially for our signature dish:
the deep-fried chicken sushi with the tempura
potatoes in a basket. But Rio wasn't sure about
the health and safety implications of having a
deep fat fryer at the diner's actual table. And
Jay-Z got cold feet, apparently because Beyonce's
people have got her tied to a long-term megadeal
with KFC back in the States and, as a couple,
they can't get their fingers in any more deep-
fried pies for the time being. I never actually met
Jay-Z as such, but that's how Rio explained it,
and sadly both he and Coley also decided to go
in a different direction.

On the plus side, me, Dexter Blackstock and
Gary Wilmot are going to give the concept a
go, so keep your eyes out for Oi! Sushi Basket
coming to a town near you soon.

FRIENDSHIP

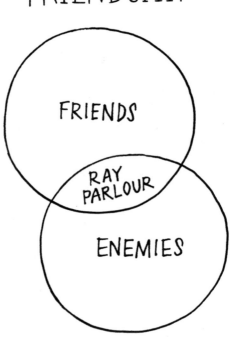

IF you talk to players, they'll tell you that the banter is what you miss most once you're finished – even more than the money. One of my best mates in football is MC Harvey, a very talented musician, defender, producer and all-round top geezer who I played with at Aldershot Town. I helped Harvs with his positioning at corners; he pulled a few strings and I had a spell on backing gunshot noises with So Solid Crew. Sadly it never worked out long term because Harvs went off to do 'Daddy Cool' in the West End and I left the UK garage collective shortly after, ironically to go on loan to Crewe. But Harvs is a true friend, and we know we'll always be there for each other.

But I've had my downs as well as ups with mates in football: take Ray Parlour. The Romford Pele and I were as thick as thieves for years – and who generously offered Ray a rent-free bunk-down in our garage when he was feeling the financial pinch after his divorce? Ronnie Matthews, that's who. And where was Ray when I had my own financial problems a few years later when the tanning salon went pear-shaped? Nowhere, that's where.

Buddha teaches you to 'let go'. All I can say is, he probably never met Ray Parlour.

EDUCATION

I WAS that bad as a kid they would have
expelled me from the school of hard knocks.
But when you have children yourself, you just
want them not to make the same mistakes you
did. Obviously it's unlikely Ginseng will ever do
time in Turkey for inciting a riot at a Galatasaray
match. And you'd have to reckon it's long odds
against that Ronnie Junior will be thrown out of
the Question of Sport green room for misreading
the signals from Tanni Grey-Thompson. But I
want them to get a proper education and not
fall into the traps I did: pride, pig-headedness,
stubbornness, drink driving.

I do a lot of promotional work these days, and to
be honest most of it goes straight on the school
fees. But if I'm ever having a hard time getting
enthusiastic about opening a sports shop with
Porky Parry or knocking a medium-sized regional
estate agents' AGM dead with my after-dinner
blue material (very reasonable rates – just drop
the publishers a line) then I just think of little
Ginseng and Ronnie Junior studying hard at
Saint Gareth's, Hemel Hempstead, and it all feels
worthwhile.

I clowned around in school, and it wasn't until later in life that I started to educate myself. You name an audiobook that's come out in the last few years, and I've probably listened to it. I usually like history and biographies, sometimes of sportsmen, sometimes great generals. If you take something like a Tony Adams then you get it all in one package.

I've got so into books actually that I was even approached to be a lecturer in The Literature of Football at the University of South Lincolnshire. Obviously with time commitments I am currently just doing guest postal lectures, and sometimes if I don't have time to actually write a letter I'll just do a Tweet, but it feels pretty good to be giving something back to the next generation. I just wish Ronnie Matthews had had a Ronnie Matthews type to keep him on the straight and narrow in his own school days. I'm like a poacher turned gamekeeper, but intellectual.

I WAS ALWAYS GETTING CANED AT SCHOOL

HEROES

I'VE always looked up to my heroes. While the other lads at Watford were sticking Louise Redknapp in their lockers, I was getting by with a picture of Harry in his training shorts.

Of course, heroes come in all shapes and sizes. I just hope some little boy out there has a Ronnie Matthews-shaped hole in his heart that I can fill.

POSSESSIONS

TAKE Arsenal: they might have all the possession, but that doesn't necessarily mean they win. Life's a bit like that too. You think you need all this stuff but when the fat lady sings at the end of the day, you can't take it with you. As I get older I realise that I don't need half of the stuff I thought I did. In fact, I reckon I could get through life with just:

Lucky number 36 shirt

Couple of pairs of shorts

Boots

My dogs

Tonette (obviously not a possession as such – it's not the 1980s)

Small car

Small car for Tonette to do the school run, go Tescos etc

Books

Paper

Pens

iPad

Actually probably could do without iPad if had
decent phone

Decent phone

Teddy bear from childhood, Hoddle (soft, I know!)

Food

Drink

House

Couple of suits for going out in, court etc

Sky TV

Headphones for wearing on coach

Bottle opener

Half set of golf clubs

Accountant

MORALITY

MORALITY. Ethics. Right and wrong. Call it
what you want, the choice between good and
evil faces us every day. On the pitch, do you
go down if you're touched in the area? Do you
simulate injury to get a fellow professional sent
off? Do you simulate injury to get yourself
taken off? Is it something in the nature of
foreigners to dive or is it behaviour they learn?

Real life can be almost as complicated. What
about if you prang somebody in the car park and
nobody's watching? Is God watching? What if
you notice there's CCTV – what about then?
If you clip a wing mirror in a forest and nobody's
there did it even happen? If a bird looked
exactly like your wife and you could sleep with
her without your wife knowing, would that
be cheating? (In the case of my wife's sister, it
turns out that it was.) But is it? (Apparently it
definitely was. Women are probably more cut
and dried in that respect.)

When I was inside in Turkey I had a lot of time
for reading. Sadly most of the books were in
Turkish, but there was a few Jeffrey Archers,
and after a couple of weeks my brief managed to

get me a stock of other books under the Geneva Convention because they said that the Archers was a cruel and unusual punishment. I actually wrote to Jeffrey and suggested Cruel And Unusual Punishment as a possible title for his next blockbuster but I never had a reply.

They sent me bibles, the Koran, Kant, Nietzsche, 'Eat Pray Love'. The classics. I devoured the philosophy books, sometimes literally when the food was especially bad, and I found that the bigger and heavier a book the more I liked it. Not just for reading but for putting down the back of your trousers as an insurance policy against certain situations that I won't go into here.

I learned that we are all moral agents, apart from football agents obviously, and that has really stuck with me ever since. We all have choices. Be the man you want to be. Don't stop believing. You can get it if you really want. Here are some of the questions that keep me awake at night:

Dive or stay on your feet?

Shoot or pass?

Truth or dare?

Stick or twist?

Chips or baked potato?

THE DRESSING ROOM

A FOOTBALL dressing room is a sacred place, and not just with all the foreign lads that have come into the game with their pre-match Hail Marys and prayers to Mecca. For a young lad breaking into the first team, it's an intimidating place. Here's the dos and don'ts I learned.

DO join in the practical jokes. When I got my England cap, I made sure the first thing I did when I got in the legendary Wembley dressing room was flush Emile Heskey's watch down the toilet.

DON'T forget that sometimes it's better to keep your head down to start with and gauge the mood of a group of lads.

DO keep an eye on your phone at all times so that the lads aren't sending your wife, manager etc prank text messages that can be hard to explain later. No pregnant woman wants a message from her husband telling her he's run off with John O'Shea. On the upside, it actually sent Tonette into labour.

DON'T smoke in the showers, especially not weed.

DON'T put your shoes on without checking in them first. I've lost count of the number of times one of the lads has put a little 'present' inside. Usually dog, sometimes human.

DO work on your banter. Footballers love to take the piss, but remember that a nickname is a mark of respect. Before I was known as 'Two Rolexes' – because I used to wear two Rolexes, one on each wrist – I was known as 'Shit Boots', on account of not checking my shoe on a pre-season tour as mentioned above.

DO remember that you can always change clubs if it all gets a bit much.

PROPERTY

NIGHTMARE! Planning permission, hidden costs, fluctuations in the international cement market. I lost the lot. I might as well have just done that three hundred grand in Vegas – at least I'd have got a complimentary junior suite and a few nights out for my money.

Leave it to the professionals, is my advice. Michael Owen and Robbie Fowler might have made millions out of property but, unless you are also a pocket-sized Scouse striker with an eye for goal and a nose for flipping bungalows, take it from me and Monsieur Marx: steer well clear.

HALF-TIME

HALFWAY through the match. The book. Life.

Time for a breather.

A cup of tea. Half an orange. Check your iPhone.

Is this all there is? Nil-nil away at Preston North End on a rainy Wednesday night?

No, there's still plenty to play for. I can turn this game around. Turn my life around.

Anything can happen in the second half.

What does the future have in store for Ronnie Matthews? I sit there in the dressing room trying to read the tea leaves like Nan used to do but it's one of those pyramid things on a string. Less looking through a glass darkly, more like squinting through a perforated tea bag. Still, it's enough to glimpse a little of what's to come. Success. Failure. Success again.

As it happens, in that game I got taken off at half-time and never played another game for the club. But that's the manager's fault, not the tea bag's.

WHEN I started out, I loved the money that came from football. Who wouldn't? I was a working-class lad, doing what I loved and getting very well paid for it. Especially after I signed for Leeds in 1999.

Admittedly, it later turned out Mr Ridsdale buying me had been an administrative cock-up, but I owe that man a massive amount. In fact, he took me to court to get a lot of it back in unjustified wages. Thank God, the judge ruled that signing me on a 37-grand-a-week five-year deal was something he couldn't go back on; contract rendered illegible due to a tropical fish tank exploding on it and smudging the ink or not. It was the first time in British legal history that a football club had tried to get a refund on a player citing their statutory consumer rights but, despite an emotional statement from Ridsdale and a long campaign by BBC's Watchdog, justice was done and Ridsdale was told to dry his eyes and keep sending the cheques.

The Leeds move took me from BMW three series league into serious top-of-the-range Porsche territory: leather this, leather that, 48 CD changer in the boot, a stereo so loud it would make you shit (literally, if you turned the bass up enough).

My first hundred-grand motor. I have to admit it still feels good typing it, but to be fair Ronnie Matthews is a much less materialistic person these days. I have to be: I haven't got the money I used to.

Everyone always says it's a disgrace that the Ronnie Matthewses of this world earn in a week what a nurse makes in a year, but

a) your nurse doesn't have to maintain the lifestyle of someone like myself

ii) I've probably given more enjoyment to blokes of the UK on a Saturday than any nurse you care to name. Apart from those ones that dress as strippers and, let's face it, probably are more stripper than nurse

3) I'm on performance-related pay, effectively. If I play bad, I get dropped, my take-home goes down, eventually I'll get sold. Now correct me if I'm wrong, but they don't dock nurses their wages if the patient dies, do they? Although obviously you've got your Harold Shipmans and that mental midwife and such like, but by and large, they're coasting along happily enough while the poor sods they're treating are dropping like flies. I just hope they can look themselves in the mirror. I know Ronnie Matthews can.

SEX

RONNIE Matthews is a romantic, and he's not shy to admit it. People think that footballers are disrespectful with women, that we're only interested in one thing, that we'll hump anything that moves. In a lot of cases that is true. It was probably true of me before I met Tonette, and during that terrible period between 2008 and 2009 when I went off the rails and put our marriage under jeopardy with my secret love nest shame.

To be fair, Tonette's sister Annette has to hold her own hand up about that period, as do the minority of idiots who defied the superinjunction on Twitter, but in the end we are all older and wiser for the experience and we've moved on. Annette's made a documentary about it for Sky Arts that will hopefully put the matter to bed once and for all.

There's one other area of human, or footballer, sexuality I'd like to write about. For me, sex is about making a real, deep connection with another human being or, if you're having a threesome, another human beings.

When you look into a teammate's eyes while you're having a threesome with a girl, that moment is a bonding experience that no amount of hours on the training ground or Saturday piss-ups can match. It's like body, mind, soul, football, the lads and Little Ronnie all in perfect harmony together and Ronnie Matthews is not ashamed to say that he finds that an awesome, powerful, beautiful thing.

RELIGION

IS Ronnie Matthews religious? Is the Pope Catholic? Trick question. Unlike the Pope, I'm a big believer that you have to have an open mind when it comes to organised religion. I suppose if I had to put my beliefs in a box I'd say I was a follower of disorganised religion. I've done a lot of reading about the major world faiths and it seems to me that there's probably no perfect solution. It's like, you've got the training facilities and glamour of a Man United, but you've got Ferguson giving you the hairdryer and telling you who you can get married to. That'd be like an Islam, or one of them Christian cults in America where you have to wash your clothes in a mangle. Or you can have a much more calm, thoughtful approach but when all's said and done you're not really putting silverware on the table. Classic Arsenal and/ or Buddhism. Way I see it, at different points in your spiritual career different things are right for you, and you have to be prepared to transfer as and when. At the end of the day, I've ended up with my unique faith, colour and creed. Like, I won't eat pork on Fridays, I always know the exact direction of Mecca, China and Canterbury, and I am proud to say I am still the host of the most expensive Diwali fireworks display Cheshire has ever seen. One love, as the Rastas say. Although obviously I've never dabbled with certain herbal aspects of that particular faith!

CHARITY

PEOPLE think that footballers have it easy, but they don't see the hours we put into training in the mornings, or the annual charity afternoons with kids' hospitals etc.

Doing work for charity is a big part of what makes Ronnie Matthews who he is, and it's really nice to give something back while also boosting your profile, keeping the tax man in his box and, in certain instances, staying out of the slammer with a few hours' community service. Charities I suppport:

> The Hangnail Trust – I've always had terrible hangnails and I know only too well the misery they can cause. People think that when I wear gloves on the field I'm being poncey, but it is actually for a sound medical reason

> No Sick Kids! – umbrella organisation that is against children being ill with life-threatening diseases

Global Warming Middle East Famine Action – charity set up by me and Kieron Dyer which aims to end climate change, eliminate world hunger and bring peace to the Middle East by 2015. We're having a sponsored Xbox marathon this Christmas so dig deep

Uncle Bongo's World Of Donkeys – theme park in Hitchin where disadvantaged kids can meet disadvantaged rescue donkeys

Parents Against Escaped Disgusting Offenders – loose coalition of mums and dads in the Portsmouth area who are not afraid to take direct measures to protect their kids

The Robbie Savage Foundation – trust fund set up for Savagey in case his media career falls through

DEPRESSION

Staring through the window pane
Looking at the drops of rain
Tough day in the bookies again
My battle with depression

When they stop cheering your name
Drifting in and out the game
Why's it always me they blame?
My battle with depression

Addicted to internet porn
Documentaries by Michael Vaughan
Yankee busted: Spurs have drawn
My battle with depression

ART

WHO'S your favourite Impressionist? Picasso? Van Gogh? Mine is probably Cezanne. David James runs him pretty close but you can't beat a good Cezanne, especially those ones with the fruit.

In football they always say 'make sure you leave everything on the pitch.' So whatever I have left over I put into my paintings. Which is probably why people dig my art so much.

This is not
a football.

PHILOSOPHY

ONE way I am broadening my mind is studying the great philosophers. With the internet, you can just type in a feeling you are having and get an amazing piece of philosophy about it right away. But I like to think that little bit deeper, so I'll often wiki away until I know basically everything about the person being quoted.

Studying the greats has definitely shaped my own personal philosophy, but I don't like to be tied to one thing. Like, I'm definitely a bit Oriental in my belief you have to open your mind to be one with everything, but I'm also a big admirer of your rational Germans, who were typically well organised with their thinking. I don't like Scottish philosophers though, even Bill Shankly. But that's just a personal thing.

Obviously a lot of the great philosophers like your Platos, your Nietzsches, your Oscar Wildes, your Camuses were writing before football was invented, but in my opinion there's a lot football could teach the world about thinking and the way the universe works. It's like the famous saying: 'All that I know about life, I have learned in boots'.

VICES

I'VE always been a man of passions and if I like something, I want as much of it as I can get. It's fair to say that Ronnie Matthews has wrestled more than his share of demons in his time, and I know for a fact I wouldn't be sitting here today if it wasn't for Tony Adams and his Sporting Chance Clinic. Every single spell I've had in there has been absolutely brilliant and I cannot recommend it highly enough.

Over the years, I have had my battles with:

Drink – When I was at Celtic I was taking a hip-flask with me to training, but to be fair, in Glasgow, that's considered par for the course. But when I started bringing two hip-flasks – one of rum, the other one of puréed bananas and glacé cherries so I could mix my own banana daiquiris in the car park – I knew it was out of control.

Coke, speed, heroin, ecstasy, LSD. Whatever I could get my hands on really. I once played

120 minutes of a League Cup game thinking I was being chased by bats. The manager – who I won't name – had himself had a bad experience with brown acid in the 1960s and I think he recognised the signs. Thank God he took me off before the penalty shootout.

Horseracing

Dog racing

Yacht racing – this is serious shit, you can do a LOT of dough in no time

Virtual horseracing – I was the first footballer to lose a hundred grand in a week on this

Sex addiction – specifically masturbating

Strepsils – was addicted to these for 18 months. At first I thought it was a cold I couldn't shake but then I realised it was something much more powerful: lozenge dependency

Internet pornography

Internet shopping

These days, thanks to God and Tony, there is only one thing I am addicted to though: LIFE!

PENALTIES

Heart beating.

Ears ringing.

Mouth dry.

Placement or power?

Left   or right?

Pizza ad or national hero?

I start my run up...

DIET

ARSENE Wenger is credited with changing the way British footballers ate and discovering that pasta etc is much better for you than traditional foods such as steak and kidney pudding, fish and chips or Nandos. Now, I don't like to blow my trumpet but I actually played a part in convincing Arsene to implicate his foody French Revolution.

Shortly after Arsene took over at the Arsenal, Watford Under 17s were playing Arsenal Under 17s at Barnet's ground on a Tuesday evening. I persuaded our driver Ray to stop at the Esso garage outside Borehamwood on the way so we could get a pre-match snack. As luck would have it, Arsene pulled onto the forecourt to fill up his Renault Five, and saw me in my Hornets tracksuit coming out of the shop with a few Scotch eggs, a packet of Cadbury's Fingers, a Ginsters, a copy of Readers' Wives and a couple of bottles of Lucozade. He didn't say nothing at the time but then he often doesn't does he? Anyway we lost 11-0 which was a tough lesson for us but the very next day one of my mates who was on YTS forms at Highbury told me that Wenger had come in the canteen and gone mental about the food, saying that if he was expected to put up with players who wanted to be like that 'fat idiot at Watford' then he'd go back to France.

His dietary revolution began right away and I suppose I have always been proud to play a part. I myself got into the whole pasta thing big time, and I'd always make sure I carbo-loaded before a big game. Carbonara-loading, we used to call it. Then the whole Atkins thing came along and I tried to cut out the spaghetti and just have the no-carb-onara, but in all fairness a pint of double cream, a few eggs and some bacon bits isn't really the best preparation for sport at the top level, as I – and the cleaners – found out in the unfortunate tunnel-vomiting incident at Kenilworth Road.

During the height of the Atkins craze I'd sometimes get so faint that I'd have to have the phsyio run on with an emergency chicken breast hidden in the magic sponge, and we'd substitute the half-time oranges for chipolatas. But all things considered I reckon a balanced diet is probably the way forward so I now just do the Atkins but get it with a baked potato.

IMMORTALITY

NONE of us will be here forever, but football
gives you a shot at immortality. I might not
have a statue named after me, and I don't think
there'll ever be a Ronnie Matthews Avenue to go
with Sir Stanley Matthews Way. But at one club
at least, I'll always be remembered as long as
the game is played.

I'm talking about the Ronnie Matthews tea bar at Brentford. As it happens, I never actually played for Brentford. But I do hold the record for most own goals scored by an opposing player at Griffin Park: seven over my career and, of course, the legendary three I unfortunately bagged there in a Worthington's Cup first-round game in 1999.

Leeds had bought me from Watford in the summer and then sent me back on loan to Watford. I got my first OG just 23 seconds into the match (still a League Cup record!) when one went in off my backside from a long throw. I added another when I slipped on the turf and volleyed home from the edge of the box, and stabbed in my third just before half-time from a corner. How unlucky can you get? Graham Taylor said he had no choice and took me off before the interval. Brentford manager Ron Noades tried to bring me back on, and even offered to buy me on the spot as long as I'd keep playing for Watford.

It was humiliating if I'm honest. I didn't see the funny side at first when they renamed the corner tea bar at Griffin Park in my honour – my three OGs had made me the Bees' top scorer that season. But, as I get older and wiser, I think: you know what? They can't take that away from me.

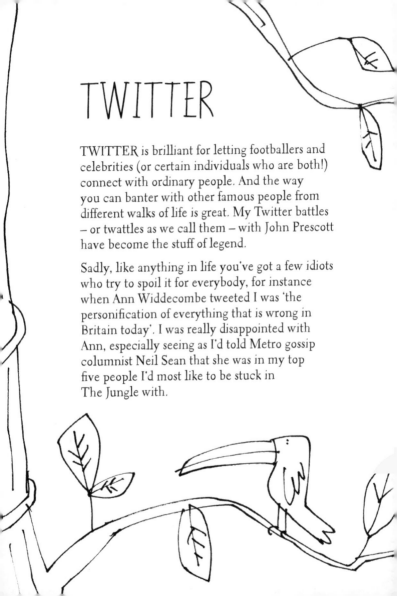

TWITTER

TWITTER is brilliant for letting footballers and celebrities (or certain individuals who are both!) connect with ordinary people. And the way you can banter with other famous people from different walks of life is great. My Twitter battles – or twattles as we call them – with John Prescott have become the stuff of legend.

Sadly, like anything in life you've got a few idiots who try to spoil it for everybody, for instance when Ann Widdecombe tweeted I was 'the personification of everything that is wrong in Britain today'. I was really disappointed with Ann, especially seeing as I'd told Metro gossip columnist Neil Sean that she was in my top five people I'd most like to be stuck in The Jungle with.

As a result of Ann's hurtful remarks I actually became a victim of cyberbullying, which is one of the most evil forms of bullying around today. Basically I became a target for a loose coalition of haters including Ann, the posh columnist Giles Coren, John Terry, the Archbishop of York and a few others, and they really put me through the online mill.

But if there is one thing I've learned in life it's to turn a positive into a negative, and I am now a spokesperson for the 'Stop. Think Before You Tweet' national campaign. We're aiming to get adverts in cinemas before films as a warning to kids, like they do with chlamydia. It's funny how life works out, because I spent most of 2006 having to pee sitting down and I had no idea what it was until we saw that advert before Big Momma's House 2. So maybe if some kid sees our advert about bullying on Twitter and stops before they say something nasty, some good will have come out of my stinging, burning sensation and Ann Widdecombe's thoughtless comments after all.

ENGLAND

I'D got on with Steve McClaren at Boro, and I was confident I'd get the nod once he got the England job. It was known Steve wanted to move on from your Beckhams and your Big Sols, and when I made the squad for an important 2007 clash I was over the moon. Even the sneering in the press – Sad Steve's wRONg Turning, Ronnie Matt-WHOs?, Sir Bobby: Matthews Selection Devalues International Football etc – couldn't dampen my spirits. The potential Faroe Islands banana skin certainly wasn't a meaningless friendly to THIS Three Lion.

As it turned out, I unfortunately became the first England player to be sent off on debut for propositioning a female linesperson, but I told myself: they can't take that cap away from me. And until an unprecedented decision by Sepp and his FIFA Europrats to retrospectively strip the match of its full international status on account of my so-called 'disgraceful actions', that was true.

Happy memories of booing the Faroe Islands national anthem aside, I've been in no doubt as to where I stand on the old club v country debate ever since.

BOO HO HO

CRIME & PUNISHMENT

YOU often hear players say: 'If it weren't for football, I'd have ended up in prison.' Well, I actually ended up in prison because of football, and if I could give one bit of advice to young footballers, I would say: enjoy the lifestyle, be a naughty boy if you have to, but do not whatever you do get banged up in Turkey.

It happened after I made by debut for Trabzonspor against Galatasaray. Because of certain activities I won't go into, I was drinking eight litres of sweet tea a day to flush out my system and avoid a ban for recreation-enhancing drugs. I was on the bench a lot, so I'd sit there drinking my tea and enjoying the sun. To be honest, I think the club only signed me to increase their media profile in the Far East. Funnily enough, I'm basically a household name in Burma. Anyway, there was an injury crisis and they had to bring me on as a sub.

I wanted to win the Turkish fans over, so at the end of the match I grabbed what I thought was a Galatasaray flag out of the crowd and mimed taking a slash on it in the centre circle. The noise from the crowd was deafening. What with the racket and all the tea, I got so overwhelmed that a bit of wee ended up coming out. That was bad, but it was only when one my teammates ran over and shouted: 'What are you doing you idiot, that's OUR flag' that I realised I'd made a huge mistake. Obviously a massive riot broke out and I was lucky to get out of there alive. If they hadn't managed to smuggle me out the ground in one of those giant bottles of Gatorade they have pitchside, I wouldn't be here today.

The club tore up my contract which, seeing as I was on a pay-as-you-play, they could do straight away. But my problems were just beginning. I was convicted of public indecency, inciting a riot and Gross Public Stupidity, which is rare in Turkish law but is pretty serious shit. They gave me nine months, and I still can't talk about my time in prison, or even look at a kebab, without terrible flashbacks. All I will say is this: stay out of trouble. In fact, probably best to stay out of Turkey altogether.

DREAMS

PARTLY to improve my understanding of myself and through that the human condition in general, and partly to see if I could get hypnotised out of compulsively buying scratchcards, I'm seeing a therapist. When I started in the game, seeking help got you called a loony and had John Gregory saying you was a disgrace to football and that his granddad worked down a mine all day and was as mad as a March hare but you never heard him complain etc etc etc. But luckily we live in a post-Collymore universe these days, and I'd go so far as to say that having a personality disorder or two has become the hot new thing in the dressing room at some clubs. All that said, I had a dream recently that freaked me out so badly I reckon I might be done with this analysis stuff for good.

I'm sitting on the settee with Tonette, watching Masterchef but when I look at her she's suddenly turned into David O'Leary. That's bad, but then she tries to pick me up and give me milk from her boobs and she's saying 'come to me moi liddle baby' in this freaky Irish accent. It's horrible. I try to run but it's like my feet are glued to the floor. I look at the TV and that Gregg Wallace article is going 'no pace at all – terrible, just terrible' but he's got Alan Hansen's voice. It's like the TV programme is in the room now and there's all these people I know in football that are the contestants in Masterchef. Ray Parlour serves his dish and goes 'I've done a lightly poached Ronnie Matthews on a bed of Ronnie Matthews' and I look at the food and it's like a miniature version of me and then everybody starts going 'that looks disgusting' but they all start eating me anyway. With chopsticks, for some reason. Then I hear a voice and it's like God but also Fergie at the same time, and he's going 'this boy'll never make a player, stick him back in at gas mark five'. I wake up screaming.

The Therapist said it was about abandonment and displaced resentment towards my mother, but I said I was sure it was about when I lent Ray Parlour a grand and he never paid me back.

And, also: say what you like about me but leave my mum out of it. Anyway, we had a row and the upshot is that I'm looking for a new therapist, so if any readers know one who's cheap and not afraid to get his hands dirty, get in touch.

MANAGEMENT

I'D definitely like to stay in football once I retire. Maybe as a pundit or like the face of an advertising campaign, but probably as a manager. I have a lot of ideas about coaching and management taken from the gaffers I have worked with or played against or seen on TV.

In my opinion the ideal manager would have:

The hairdryer of Sir Alex Ferguson – legendary. Only Gerry Francis had a better hairdryer but he started using it on his actual hair and drifted out of the game at the highest level

The compensation package of Fabio Ca- – you're only as rich as your last sackin

The laser eyes of Roy Keane – well scary in the dressing room and for getting players to sign contracts etc

The scarf of Roberto Mancini – because I'm worth it

The physical presence of Sam Allardyce – you don't mess with a manager who can eat three lamb vindaloos with the works

INJURIES

REGRETS? Sure – a bit more luck with injury would have been nice. Maybe at times I haven't helped myself, but for a while I actually begun to think I was cursed. Here's just some of the bad luck I've had:

Hyperextended wrist when trying to carry too many cones at Watford, aged 17. Bit of a recurring theme this – putting my body on the line to impress a manager.

I missed half a season as a 19-year-old with a hypersensitive tailbone.

At Leeds, I was out for three months with Listlessness. The club thought I was just lazy. Thankfully medical science has moved on a lot since then, partly in thanks to my awareness-raising work with the National Listlessness Trust.

It was the period 2007–2010 though that was my worst. I just seemed to go from one niggle to another. I had: collapsed cruciate bone displacement, dorsal fatigue, a dead arm that lasted six months, one of the worst cases of leaden feet the club doctor had ever seen, a fractured skull, recurring hangnails, gout, alcohol poisoning and paranoia.

Playing out on the wing for Hartlepool one February, I came down with micro-shrinking of the penis, which is where your old feller shrivels up so much due to the cold that in extreme cases you can actually be technically declared a woman. The lads thought that was hilarious but believe me there's nothing funny about standing in the shower crying and wondering how you're going to tell your wife that your dick's disappeared.

However, I was lucky enough to spend some time with Eileen Drury when we were both staying at the same resort in Antigua, and she had some brilliant suggestions. I've worked a lot on my chi, focused on getting more centred, and taken up yogic flying. I also now make sure that I play in one of those protective skull caps Petr Cech has, and I've had some good results with wearing the glaucoma sunglasses that Edgar Davids made famous. Along with the nasal plaster breathing strips that Robbie Fowler recommended, I now go into every game looking – and feeling – like a complete warrior.

ISMS

FOOTBALL'S been like a father to me, but
it's like a father who was born in a different
generation. Scientists reckon that dinosaurs were
wiped out by a meteor strike – all I can say to
that is: they've never been to football in the likes
of Turkey, your Bulgarias or Yorkshire.

Some of the attitudes you get in football are
disgusting. I am a passionate supporter of the
Give Isms The Elbow (GITE). It's like a splinter
group of Kick Racism Out Of Football – PFA
boss Gordon Taylor called it the 'lunatic fringe'.
That was out of order, but then that's the football
establishment for you.

GITE is a group of modern-thinking players, supporters and celebrities who have a zero-tolerance policy on Racism, Sexism, Misogynism, Homophobianism and any other Isms not yet discovered. I'm a patron, along with Garth Crooks, Graeme Le Saux, Germaine Greer, Ron Atkinson and Skin, the bald lesbianly-challenged one from Skunk Anansie.

Basically we get together once a month to raise awareness, use our media presences to highlight issues and have a charity game. Sadly, Skin recently got an 11-match ban from UEFA: she went through Big Ron with a nasty late one after Duncan from Blue gave him a hospital pass at Boundary Park. That was a shame, but we got a lot of press.

Basically Britain's a melting pot these days, and football has to catch on. There's no ism in multiculturalism. That's our motto.

THE FINAL WHISTLE

TONETTE says it's morbid but I've got my funeral all planned out. When the great referee in the sky blows for full time, Ronnie Matthews will be ready to swap shirts with the opposition, jog round the touchline applauding the fans and step into the big communal bath of the afterlife.

I wanted to be buried in a Baby Bentley but to be fair it was an insurance nightmare, and I'd put in an application to have a real proper East End funeral, even though I'm not from the East End myself, but I couldn't get planning permission. So when my time comes it will be a tasteful service with my ashes scattered at a select few of the 23 clubs I have played for professionally, with Four Poofs And A Piano providing the music. Assuming I don't outlive him, Ainsley Harriott's doing nibbles.

As I go into the incinerator they'll play 'My Way'. If I live for a long time (as I plan to!) there's a chance it might take longer to crisp me up than that song lasts because older bodies take longer to burn apparently. If so, we'll have a Lionel Richie medley so the ladies can have a bit of a cry, but in an uplifted way.

RONNIE
MATTHEWS
—
HUSBAND
FATHER
MIDFIELD DYNAMO
WITH AN EYE
FOR GOAL

EXTRA TIME

DEATH might be the end of 90 minutes, but I'm a big believer that there's always extra time – and a whole new season beginning soon after.

If a person was a football club, when their time is up, I don't reckon that they get liquidated like an Aldershot. Or, what I mean is, they do – but they can get reincarnated as an Aldershot Town. This is just a metaphor obviously.

Or maybe death is more like being relegated: you've battled all season against the drop but at the end of the day you have to hold your hand up and go down. But it's always possible to come back up, bigger and stronger than before, like a West Ham under Big Sam. In the likes of your yo-yo clubs like Birmingham or West Brom, you're in a whole karmic circle of death, rebirth and pulsating Midlands derbies on Sky Sports 1. It's actually really beautiful if you think about it.

If I was reincarnated I'd like to come back as a dog – that's probably a pretty good life – or preferably in the Gary Neville role on Monday Night Football. Or maybe you just drift away into a great big wide open nothing, filled with love and peace and playing golf, which is what I reckon it must be like being one of the Match of the Day boys.

Ronnie Matthews doesn't have the answers, but he does have a lot of questions, and he'll hopefully be asking them for a long while yet.

RESPECTS

THANKS to Alan Tyers, my ghost-writer and number-one fan for his help with the words.

Props to Beach, my life-drawing tutor, for his advice on the art and for teaching me that little trick with the tippex.

Big shout out to Charlotte at the publishing company for going the extra mile and busting the Bloomsbury wage structure to sign me up. Thanks for keeping it real, babes.

And of course massive thanks to Tonette and the kids for giving me the time and space to write this book. It can't have been easy for them being without their Dad for such long spells that weekend. The next one will be quicker, I promise.

And lastly, thanks to the fans. You know who you are.

Peace out.